A Sense of Belonging
Six Scottish Poets of the Seventies

D1322191

A Sense of Belonging
Six Scottish Poets of the Seventies

Compiled by Brian Murray and Sydney Smyth

. . . It is hard to look
Back with any sense of belonging.
Too much has changed, is still changing.

STEWART CONN, 'On Craigie Hill'

Blackie & Son Ltd
Bishopbriggs, Glasgow G64 2NZ
450 Edgware Road, London W2 1EG

© This collection
Brian Murray and Sydney Smyth 1977
First published 1977
Educational edition   ISBN 0 216 90264 9
General edition   ISBN 0 216 90369 6

Contents

STEWART CONN

Tremors

We took turns at laying
An ear on the rail—
So that we could tell
By the vibrations

When a train was coming.
Then we'd flatten ourselves
To the banks, scorched
Vetch and hedge-parsley,

While the iron flanks
Rushed past, sending sparks
Flying. It is more and more
A question of living

With an ear to the ground:
The tremors, when they come,
Are that much greater—
For ourselves, and others.

Nor is it any longer
A game, but a matter
Of survival: each explosion
Part of a procession

There can be no stopping.
Though the end is known,
There is nothing for it
But to keep listening . . .

Portents

Southpark
The area palls, and its mildewed parades.
    Victorian terraces,
  Taken over for the University, lose
Their ironwork, their fluted balustrades.

Among the charred bedsteads, the crazy mirrors,
    I keep thinking of those men in dungarees
  Putting an axe through Mackintosh's
Front door . . . Glasgow is in arrears.

The Salon
The supporting programme always began
At 5.30. But they didn't open
      Till 5.28. So that
  By the time you'd got your ticket
      And found your seat
You'd missed the first four minutes.

Once when we could scarcely see the screen
    For fog, we didn't complain—
  But sat through the entire programme again:
    Phantom cops, after a phantom Keaton.

    In December, the gate
    Was locked. The white
Frontage peels. The posters are gone
But for a clutch of curls, a crimped grin.

Costume Piece
Every morning, two women in Edwardian costume
Stood for hours opposite the men's Union.

It seemed one or other had been let down
By a medical student: clear water over sharp stones.

When they disappeared, I hoped for a happy
Conclusion—only to hear both had been put away.

Botanics
Somewhere, a clock strikes. Schoolboys
    In cherry caps and corduroys
Face the deathtrap of Great Western Road
    Watched by a lollipop-man; then head

For the ice-cream parlour
    And the Gardens—where the keeper,
Not wanting trouble, goes inside
    To his prize orchids, his marble nudes.

Behind the hothouse the boys shout
    At an artist in sombrero and tights
Too dour even to look up. By the gate
    The winnowing fantails preen and pirouette.

Choral Symphony

The customary conversation
Gives way to applause
For the Orchestra. Then
A roar, as Karajan
Takes the stand. He raises
His baton: the strings sweep in.

During the interval, we remain
Seated. Two Edinburgh ladies
Behind us complain:
'Such Teutonic discipline
Breeds perfection,
Not Art.' Their companion agrees.

At the end they join in,
As the ovation goes on
And on. What has changed their tune?
We overhear: 'Weren't the Chorus
Superb!' 'As one voice.'
'And that lace, on Muriel's dress.'

Winter

Part of the Bay seemed to freeze.
Between here and the Point
Was suspended a curtain
Of spray, a frill of silk.

Birds wintered here, blown
Off course. A spoonbill,
Taken on one of the skerries,
Was sent to the museum—

Its breast shot away. 'Worst
Since '41, when two smacks
Had their keels crushed and the Tink
Was found, hands stuck

To a metal drum.' I concede
Things were worse in those days.
Nevertheless I take
What they say with a pinch

Of salt—knowing how in time
I shall describe this
Winter's glory: ice to the Kame,
The seals surfacing with ruffs of lace.

Alridge Pond

To this salt-water enclosure
Came families of fin-whales,
Anything up to eighty tons, superior
In hunting method to our sonar.
Turning their underbellies to the light
They'd herd the herring closer and closer
Then take what food they wanted.
Till one January, the herring in glut,
A pregnant mother-whale entered
An inlet she could not have navigated

But for the spring tide. Her mate,
Unable to join her, drove shoal upon shoal
Into the pool where she had been caught.
What a chance for the conservationists,
The marine biologists. Their help never
Came. After four days 400 nickel bullets
Were bedded in her body; a motor-boat's blade
Had cut a swathe from her side. The fishermen
Saw in her perhaps an exemplar
Of their own servitude. Some wanted
To preserve her till the height
Of the tourist season. None ministered
To the sores that finally festered.

They towed her, by the tail, out to sea
Where she floated easily, borne
By the gases of her own dissolution.

In the Kibble Palace

In the Kibble Palace with its dazzling statues
And glass dome, reading a poet I've just come across,
I learn that under the ice the killer whale

Seeing anything darker than snow, falls away
Then charges, smashing the ice with his forehead,
Isolating seal or man on a drifting piece

Of the floe. Imagine those tons of blubber
Thrusting up; tail curvetting
As the hammer head hits. What if the skull

Should split, splinters penetrate to the brain?
Nor will dry land protect us from the thudding
In the blood, these forces below. How can we conquer

Who cannot conquer ourselves? I shall think of this
When, fishing on frosted glass, I find
My line tightening against the swell;

Or, hearing you moan and turn in your sleep,
I know you are on your own, far out,
Dark shapes coursing below. Meanwhile

The horizon closes in, a glass
Globe. We will admit it is there
When it is too late; and blunder for the exits

To find them locked. Seeing as though through ice
Blurred forms gyrate, we will put our heads
Together and try to batter a way out.

Forbears

My father's uncle was the fastest
Thing on two wheels, sitting in a gig,
The reins tight, his back at an angle
Of thirty degrees, puffing up dust-clouds
And he careered down Craigie Hill.

His father before him, the strongest man
In Ayrshire, took a pair of cartwheels
By the axle and walked off with them. I have
Visions of him in the meadow, holding
Two ropes, a stallion straining on each.

Before that, no doubt, we boasted
The straightest furrow, the richest yield.
No measurement needed: each farm
Bore its best, as each tree its fruit.
We even had a crazy creature in crinolines

Who locked her letters in a brass box.
Others too . . . But what do such truths
Add up to—when the nearest
(And furthest) I get is visiting
Their elaborate, uncared-for graves?

On an adjoining stone are a skull
And hourglass, from Covenanter
Days. Their lives were a duller
Sacrifice. John on his moral staff,
The great-aunts with their rigid ways,

Smacking of goodness in the strictest
Sense, members of a sect, Elect almost,
Shared surely something of flint
In the brain. Sad, that their mortal goal
Was salvation, not purification of the soul.

On Craigie Hill

The farmhouse seems centuries ago,
The steadings slouched under a sifting of snow
For weeks on end, lamps hissing, logs stacked
Like drums in the shed, the ice having to be cracked
To let the shaggy cats drink. Or
Back from the mart through steaming pastures
Men would come riding—their best
Boots gleaming, rough tweeds pressed
To a knife-edge, pockets stuffed with notes.

Before that even, I could visualize (from coloured
Prints) traps rattling, wheels spinning; furred
Figures posing like sepia dolls
In a waxen world of weddings and funerals.
When Todd died, last of the old-stagers,
Friends of seventy years followed the hearse.
Soon the farm went out of the family: the Cochranes
Going to earth or, like their cousins,
Deciding it was time to hit town.

The last link broken, the farm-buildings stand
In a clutter below the quarry. The land
Retains its richness—but in other hands.
Kilmarnock has encroached. It is hard to look
Back with any sense of belonging.

Too much has changed, is still changing.
This blustery afternoon on Craigie Hill
I regard remotely the muddy track
My father used to trudge along, to school.

To My Father

One of my earliest memories (remember
Those Capone hats, the polka-dot ties)
Is of the late thirties: posing
With yourself and grandfather before
The park railings; me dribbling
Ice-cream, you so spick and smiling
The congregation never imagined
How little you made. Three generations,
In the palm of a hand. A year later
Grandfather died. War was declared.

In '42 we motored to Kilmarnock
In Alec Martin's Terraplane Hudson.
We found a pond, and six goldfish
Blurred under ice. They survived
That winter, but a gull got them in the end.
Each year we picnicked on the lawn;
Mother crooking her finger
As she sipped her lime. When
They carried you out on a stretcher
She knew you'd never preach again.

Since you retired, we've seen more
Of each other. Yet I spend this forenoon
Typing, to bring you closer—when
We could have been together. Part of what
I dread is that clear mind nodding
Before its flickering screen. If we come over
Tonight, there will be the added irony
Of proving my visit isn't out of duty
When, to myself, I doubt the dignity
Of a love comprising so much guilt and pity.

Reiteration

What terrifies me is that you should see your death
Reflected in my eyes. Yours are moist, glazed
Over; rimmed with red, as you gaze
At the images on their tiny screen. Beneath

The surface of things, your heart takes
Irregular leaps forward, toward the dark.
Its rhythms are broken easily; by the van parked
Too close for comfort, the fool whose brakes

Took him through the Argyle Street
Lights; Lennox's goal in the dying minutes . . .
And I think of the pressures youth puts
On age, neither prepared to meet

The other half-way. I remember you beat
Me, with a leather belt, for using a word
That can nowadays be overheard
Even in your trim Bearsden street.

I swore I'd get my own back
When I was older, stronger;
I'd wait till you no longer
Had the upper hand, and give you an attack

One way or another. Now I see
How strengths vary; the grasp
Of one over another depending not on the clasp
Of wrist or forearm. You are still stronger than me—

And apart from all else, have more experience
Of death's ways, having watched others go.
Here in this tiny space, you
Stare calmly at what I only dimly sense.

Far from being imprisoned in this room,
Which is how I'd seen it, the big guns
Thudding, I realize you've won
More battles than most—and have just one to come.

Family Visit

Laying linoleum, my father spends hours
With his tape measure,
Littering the floor
As he checks his figures, gets
The angle right; then cuts
Carefully, to the music
Of a slow logic. In despair
I conjure up a room where
A boy sits and plays with coloured bricks.

My mind tugging at its traces,
I see him in more dapper days
Outside the Kibble Palace
With my grandfather, having
His snapshot taken; men firing
That year's leaves.
The Gardens are only a stone's throw
From where I live . . . But now
A younger self comes clutching at my sleeve.

Or off to Innellan, singing, we would go,
Boarding the steamer at the Broomielaw
In broad summer, these boomps-a-daisy
Days, the ship's band playing in a lazy
Swell, my father steering well clear
Of the bar, mother making neat
Packets of waste-paper to carry
To the nearest basket or (more likely)
All the way back to Cranworth Street.

Leaving my father at it
(He'd rather be alone) I take
My mother through the changed Botanics.
The bandstand is gone, and the great
Rain-barrels that used to rot
And overflow. Everything is neat
And plastic. And it is I who must walk
Slowly for her, past the sludge
And pocked marble of Queen Margaret Bridge.

DOUGLAS DUNN

White Fields

An aeroplane, its red and green night-lights
Spotting its distant noise in the darkness;
'Jack Frost,' you say, pointing to white fields
Sparkling. My eyes accept the dark, the fields
Extend, spreading and drifting, fences rising
Before the black hedge that zips beside the road
I'm told I must never try to cross without you.
'What time is it?'—'The middle of the night!
You've had a dream, I heard you shout.'
It woke me and I cried aloud, until
My mother came and showed me the farm
Wasn't burning, the school still had its roof,
There was no one hidden in the little fir trees.
'Only an aeroplane!' As if you meant by that
That there in 1948 in Renfrewshire
We were safe from fear, and the white eyes
Of dead Jews were just photographs
In a terrible past, a neighbour's magazine.
'Only an aeroplane!' Unsleeping factories,
All night you busied overhead, and flames
Flushed out my cities made of shoe-boxes
And dominoes, my native village of shaws.
So innocent machine! I had a toy like you
That I made buzz and drone like Leiper's bees,
From which I dropped the A-bomb on John's pram,
Crumpling the hand-embroidered sheets.
    Our breath melted ice on the window-pane.
Fields drizzled on the glass, opening strips
Of short-lived clarity, and fingernails of ice
Slid to the sill. 'No harm will come to us.'
I slept. Till now I've slept, dreaming of mice
Burrowing under the crusted tufts of snow
That heaviest fall had left us with,
Our planet flooded into continents
Of stray, white islands, a sea too cold to swim.
Till now I've slept, and waking, I reject

Your generation, an old copy of *Everybody's*
Thrown out with *Film Fun* and the tea-leaves,
Bulldozed by a conscript from our village
Into a pit dug by forced labour.
So easily is love shed, I hardly feel it.

   White fields, your angled frost filed sharply
Bright over undisturbed grasses, do not soothe
As similes of innocence or idle deaths
That must happen anyway, an unmoral blankness;
Be unforgiving stillness, natural, what is:
Crimes uttered in landscape, smoke-darkened snow.

   Trains in my distance altered. Cattle trucks
Seemed to chug through Georgetown, a station
Where a fat man in a black uniform kept hens
On the platform: but the waggons sprouted arms
And dropped dung, and no one sang
'Ten Green Bottles' or 'The Sash'. Offensive outings.

Six years old! And I lived through the worst of it!

Boys with Coats

When I was ten, outside the Govan Plaza,
My first day on the Glasgow Underground,
I gave a boy with no coat in the sleet and rain
My pocket-money and my model aeroplane.
He said he was going to Greenock, the place
For which our bus was named, 'via Inchinnan'
Where we lived in village comfort near
An aerodrome—HMS *Sanderling*,
Its concrete fields of war named for a bird
I'd never seen. 'My father's in Greenock,'
He said; but the conductress wouldn't let him on.
Faces through streaming windows stared contempt
To see him set off in the wet to Linthouse
Where they all guessed he lived—the tenements
That frightened me because they were so dark.

I who had sat in Monty's staff car at the Motor Show,
Having been born on the night of Alamein
In the war that serving justice served injustice—
That children with coats might give to those without,
Effacing rights of ownership with gifts—
Felt radical that my lost Hurricane
Solved nothing in the sleet and rain.

The Competition

When I was ten, going to Hamilton
On the Leyland bus named for Eddlewood,
A boy with an aeroplane just like mine
Zoomed at his war games in the seat in front.
I'd never seen such a school uniform—
As brown as the manure in Cousar's coup
Where someone's city cousin had jumped in
Having been told it was 'just sand'—
One of Glasgow's best fee-paying places,
Brown as barrowloads from the blue-bottled byre.
I couldn't help it; I had to talk to him
And tell him I, too, had a Hurricane.
His mother pulled him to her, he sat sullen,
As if I'd spoiled his game. I spoke again,
And he called me a poor boy, who should shut up.
I'd never thought of it like that.
The summer tenements were so dry I cried.
My grandfather wouldn't give *him* sixpence.

Years later, running in a race, barefooted
As I'd trained my spikes to ruin, convinced
My best competitor was him, I ran into
The worst weathers of pain, determined to win,
But on the last lap, inches from the tape, was beaten
By someone from Shotts Miners Welfare Harriers Club.

After the War

The soldiers came, brewed tea in Snoddy's field
Beside the wood from where we watched them pee
In Snoddy's stagnant pond, small boys hidden
In pines and firs. The soldiers stood or sat
Ten minutes in the field, some officers apart
With the select problems of a map. Before,
Soldiers were imagined, we were them, gunfire
In our mouths, most cunning local skirmishers.
Their sudden arrival silenced us. I lay down
On the grass and saw the blue shards of an egg
We'd broken, its warm yolk on the green grass,
And pine cones like little hand grenades.

One burst from an imaginary Browning,
A grenade well thrown by a child's arm,
And all these faces like our fathers' faces
Would fall back bleeding, trucks would burst in flames,
A blood-stained map would float on Snoddy's pond.
Our ambush made the soldiers laugh, and some
Made booming noises from behind real rifles
As we ran among them begging for badges,
Our plimsolls on the fallen May-blossom
Like boots on the faces of dead children.
But one of us had left. I saw him go
Out through the gate, I heard him on the road
Running to his mother's house. They lived alone,
Behind a hedge round an untended garden
Filled with broken toys, abrasive loss;
A swing that creaked, a rusted bicycle.
He went inside just as the convoy passed.

Ships

When a ship passes at night on the Clyde,
Swans in the reeds, picking oil from their feathers,
Look up at the lights, the noise of new waves
Against hill-climbing houses, malefic cranes.

A fine rain attaches itself to the ship like skin.
Lascars play poker, the Scottish mate looks
At the last lights, one that is Ayrshire,
Others on lonely rocks, or clubfooted peninsulas.

They leave restless boys without work in the river towns.
In their houses are fading pictures of fathers ringed
Among ships' complements in wartime, model destroyers,
Souvenirs from uncles deep in distant engine rooms.

Then the boys go out, down streets that look on water.
They say, 'I could have gone with them,'
A thousand times to themselves in the glass cafés,
Over their American soft drinks, into their empty hands.

Bring Out Your Dead

A cart goes by, the creaking wheels of peace,
Loaded up with old cookers and discarded clothes.
The widows finally threw out their husbands' suits,
On their way to decadence, remarriage, or classic grief.

The driver sings, a child teases him with an old boot.
Man and boy, they take away the used, discarded heap.
A widow looks in an empty wardrobe, at mothballs
Like old fondant sweets, a pair of shoes she missed.

Men of Terry Street

They come in at night, leave in the early morning.
I hear their footsteps, the ticking of bicycle chains,
Sudden blasts of motorcycles, whimpering of vans.
Somehow I am either in bed, or the curtains are drawn.

This masculine invisibility makes gods of them,
A pantheon of boots and overalls.
But when you see them, home early from work
Or at their Sunday leisure, they are too tired

And bored to look long at comfortably.
It hurts to see their faces, too sad or too jovial.
They quicken their step at the smell of cooking,
They hold up their children and sing to them.

A Removal from Terry Street

On a squeaking cart, they push the usual stuff,
A mattress, bed ends, cups, carpets, chairs,
Four paperback westerns. Two whistling youths
In surplus U.S. Army battle-jackets
Remove their sister's goods. Her husband
Follows, carrying on his shoulders the son
Whose mischief we are glad to see removed,
And pushing, of all things, a lawnmower.
There is no grass in Terry Street. The worms
Come up cracks in concrete yards in moonlight.
That man, I wish him well. I wish him grass.

Wedding

Confetti in the gutters,
Half a dozen leaves
That reach here from autumn,
Yearly . . . What point is there
In regretting no shrubbery
Or abundance of green
Hallows this couple, when the car
The groom has worked on for weeks
Takes them down a street
Elated by love and community?
There is one season
For poverty, and delight
Overlaps all things.

The Silences

It is urban silence, it is not true silence.
The main road, growling in the distance,
Continuous, is absorbed into it;
The birds, their noises become lost in it;
Faint, civilized music decorates it.

These are edges round a quiet centre where lives are lived,
Children brought up, where television aerial fixers come,
Or priests on black bikes to lecture the tardy.
If you turn your back on it, people are only noises,
Coughs, footsteps, conversations, hands working.

They are a part of the silence of places,
The people who live here, working, falling asleep,
In a place removed one style in time outwith
The trend of places. They are like a lost tribe.
The dogs bark when strangers come, with rent books, or
    free gifts.

They move only a little from where they are fixed.
Looking at worn clothes, they sense impermanence,
They have nothing to do with where they live, the silence
    tells them.
They have looked at it so long, with such disregard,
It is baked now over their eyes like a crust.

TOM LEONARD

Poetry

the pee as in pulchritude,
oh pronounced ough
as in bough

the ee rather poised
(pronounced ih as in wit)
then a languid high tea . . .

pause: then the coda—
ray pronounced rih
with the left eyebrow raised
—what a gracious bouquet!

Poetry.
Poughit. rih.

That was my education
—and nothing to do with me.

Words, for E

The sky is blue, or something. Anyway it's there.
Your words are hands, stroking me, stroking the sky.
Blue sky, names, people. It's marvellous—I'm king,
And your words are a line of ships. The guns fire.
Blue sky, names, people. I take the salute.

You are beautiful, sometimes. Now.
I feel for words for you. The ship rising, falling,
The horizon, a line rising, falling, behind your hair.
Words rise, spray. I like to think of you as giving
Structure. A gentleness. A constancy.

A Summer's Day

yir eyes ur
eh
a mean yir

pirrit this wey
ah a thingk yir
byewtifl like ehm

fact
fact a thingk yir
ach a luvyi thahts

thahts
jist thi wey it iz like
thahts ehm
aw ther iz ti say

The Appetite

That conversation was a tread,
a trampoline. 'Words are absurd',
it said, and our eyes played
at not being on it, laughing.

We sat facing each other, eating
as if
we sat facing each other, eating.

Moral Philosophy

whiji *mean* whiji mean

lissn
noo lissnty mi toknty yi
right

h hawd oan
whair wuzza
naw

aye
whitsiz name
him way thi
yi no yon

here
here yoo
yir no eevn lissnin
name a god

a doant no

The Good Thief

heh jimmy
yawright ih
stull wayz urryi
ih

heh jimmy
ma right insane yirra pape
ma right insane yirwanny uz jimmy

see it nyir eyes
wanny uz

heh

heh jimmy
lookslik wirgonny miss thi gemm
gonny miss thi GEMM jimmy
nearly three a cloke thinoo

dork init
good jobe theyve gote thi lights

Fireworks

up cumzthi wee man
beats three men
slingzowra crackir

an Lennux
aw yi wahntia seenim
coolizza queue cumbir

bump

rightnthi riggin
poastij stamp
a rockit

that wuzzit
that wuzthi end

finisht

Yon Night

yonwuz sum night
thi Leeds gemmit Hamdin
a hunnirn thurty four thousan
aw singin
yilnivir wok alone

wee burdnma wurk then
nutsnur a wuz
but she wuzny intristid
yi no thi wey

well there wuzza stonnin
ana wuz thaht happy
ana wuz thaht fed up
hoffa mi wuz greetnaboot Celtic
anhoffa mi wuz greetnaboot hur

big wain thata wuz
a kin laffitit noo

Jiss Ti Let Yi No
(from the American of Carlos Williams)

ahv drank
thi speshlz
that wurrin
thi frij

n thit
yiwurr probbli
hodn back
furthi pahrti

awright
they wur great
thaht stroang
thaht kawld

The Dropout

scrimpt nscraipt furryi
urryi grateful
no wan bit

speylt useless yi urr
twistid izza coarkscrew
cawz rowz inan empty hooss

yir fathir nivirid yoor chance
pick n choozyir joab
a steady pey

well jiss take a lookit yirsell
naithur wurk nur wahnt
aw aye

yir clivir
damm clivir
but yi huvny a clue whutyir dayn

Paroakial

thahts no whurrits aht
thahts no cool man
jiss paroakial

aw theez sporran heads
tahty scoan vibes
thi haggis trip

bad buzz man
dead seen

goahty learna new langwij
sumhm ihnturnashnl
noah Glasgow hangup
bunnit husslin

gitinty elektroniks man
really blow yir mine
real good blast
no whuhta mean

mawn
turn yirself awn

The Qualification

wurk aw yir life
nuthnty show
pit oanthi nyuze
same awl drivl

yoonyin bashn
wurkir bashn
lord this
sir soan soa thaht

shood hearma boay
sayzwi need gunz
an armd revalooshn
nuthn else wurks

awright fur him thoa
uppit thi yooni
tok aw yi like therr
thats whit its fur

The Other Side of the Ticket

I have quoted the number of deaths in obscure battles
In order to pass examinations; I have quoted the number
Of deaths in more recent disasters, that some life might
Be brought to a dying conversation; I have been moved by
Animated discussions in restaurants on the question of
World famine; I have shuffled in anxious queues that
Could not wait to see the authentic films of the tortured
Under the Nazi rule, and I have listened to the satisfied
Shocked voices, and agreed that it was terrible to watch;
I have fled from Pacifists, beside themselves with rage;
I have befriended people with or without pamphlets and
Badges, whose logic would hammer its fist on the table,
Or announce itself in a rush of words when an innocent
Topic was introduced: I have watched them fumbling along
Their narrow lanes, scrawling on the high brick walls on
Either side that God is Love, or that God does not exist
At all, or whatever the motto transcribed from the gleam
In their eyes. But I have laughed, being myself for once,
On having picked up a newspaper with its frantic reasons
For despair, joy, or national pride, and having realized
That only the crossword had changed from the previous day.
And bored with sincerity, the drunkard's tight grip on
The lapel, I have returned to the Nazi film to jeer at
The wide-eyed crowds, and been thrown out, clutching
My ticket that thanked me and asked me to come again.

LIZ LOCHHEAD

Lady of Shalott

Fifteen or younger
she moons in the mirror.
Penny for your thoughts,
Lady of Shalott.

In her bedroom tower
with mother and father
watching T.V. downstairs,
she moons in the mirror
and swears she will never
lead a bloody boring life like theirs.

Maybe you'll find True Romance
at the youth club dance,
Lady of Shalott.

She paints her nails scarlet,
she moons in the mirror.
Ingenue or harlot?
The mirror is misted,
every mirror image twisted.
Like Real Life—but larger.
That kid-glove
dream love
a Knight on a Charger.
Sure
you can lure
him, keep him enslaved.
Buy him Christmas aftershave.

She moons in the mirror
asks it to tell her
she's every bit as pretty as the other
gadfly girls.
Yes, you'll tangle him in your curls
my Lady of Shalott.

Maybe tonight's the night for
True Romance.
You'll find him at the youth club dance,
Lady of Shalott.

But alas
no handsome prince to dare
ask Rapunzel to let down her hair.
Her confidence cracked from side to side,
by twelve o'clock her tattered pride
is all Cinders stands in.
You're the wallflower the fellows all forgot,
Lady of Shalott.
Oh, how she wishes she could pass
like Alice through the looking glass.
You're waiting to be wanted,
my fairy-tale haunted
Lady of Shalott.

Silver dance shoes in her pocket,
no one's photo in her locket,
home alone through the night,
on either side suburban gardens lie,
bungalows and
bedded boxed-in couples high and dry.
But you're
lovely in the lamplight,
my Lady of Shalott.

Bawd

I'll get all dolled up in my gladrags, stay
up till all hours, oh
up to no good.
It'll amaze you, the company I keep
(and I'll keep them at arm's length).
I've hauled my heart in off my sleeve.

I'll let my hair down,
go blonde, be a bombshell, be on the make.
I'll gold dig, I'll be frankly fake.

I'll paint my face up, paint the town,
have carmine nails, oh
be a fatal dame.
I've bold eyes, kohl sockets.
I'll look daggers, kill.
My lipstick colour's Merry Hell.

I'd frighten the French.
I'll be a torment, haunt men's dreams,
I'll wear my stockings black with seams.

I'll rouge my cleavage, flaunt myself, my heels
will be perilously high, oh
but I won't sway.
I'll shrug everything off the shoulder,
make wisecracks, be witty off the cuff.
Tell blue jokes in mixed company.

I'll be a bad lot.
I've a brass neck. There is mayhem in my smile.
No one will guess it's not my style.

Song

My father
would warn of the danger. Eggs all
in one basket. Pride hurtling for its fall.
One swallow does not make a summer,
he'd have me remember.

I'm seven, I'm
over the moon.
I've a brand new coat of bright red stuff.
My father asks me is it warm enough.

I'm twenty four, I
go over the score.
In my father's eyes I'm all but lost.
I want magenta and pentecost.

This letter
is from my father. He forwards mail and
drops a quick line in his careful hand.
How am I for money? Am I sure I've enough?
Father forgive. Though it's hard to see,
                                        you sign 'with love'.

My Rival's House

is peopled with many surfaces.
Ormolu and gilt, slipper satin,
lush velvet couches,
cushions so stiff you can't sink in,
tables polished clear enough to see distortions in.

We take our shoes off at her door,
shuffle stocking-soled, tiptoe—the parquet floor
is beautiful and its surface must
be protected. Dust-
cover, drawn shade.
Won't let the surface colour fade.

Silver sugar tongs and silver salver
my rival serves us tea.
She glosses over him and me.
I am all edges, a surface, a shell
and yet my rival thinks she means me well.
But what swims beneath her surface I can tell.
Soon, my rival
capped tooth, polished nail
will fight, fight foul for her survival.
Deferential, daughterly, I sip
and thank her nicely for each bitter cup.

And I have much to thank her for.
This son she bore—
first blood to her—
never, never, never can escape scot free
from the sour pot-luck of family.
And oh how close
this family that furnishes my rival's place.
Lady of the house.
Queen bee.
She is far more unconscious
far more dangerous than me.
Listen, I was always my own worst enemy.
She has taken even this from me.

She dishes up her dreams for breakfast.
Dinner and her salt tears pepper our soup.
She won't give up.

Bluejohn Pockets
(Bluejohn is a stone found in the limestone
caves in Derbyshire's Peak District)

You came to the city.
You came to see me
bringing me driftwood you found by the sea.
One night in my tower
and the next thing I knew
I was out on the motorway hitching with you.
Next to nothing in our pockets
to live on.

It wasn't so always.
Not you and me.
And once this mountain lay under the sea.
Look close at the surface
you can easily tell
how it changed how it hardened to fossilized shell
that lies in deep caves by the pockets
of bluejohn.

Bluejohn oh bluejohn
marbled and scarred
blue bright and hard
oh it runs like a vein through the rock seam.
Never a day but you think of her
and I of him.

Back now in the city,
what can I save
but this mantelpiece full of the bluejohn you gave.
Yes we each loved another,
but times have moved on.
Ask me once to go with you, I'll be packed up and gone
with nothing in my pockets
but bluejohn.

Bluejohn oh bluejohn
marbled and scarred
blue bright and hard
oh it runs like a vein through the rock seam.
Never a day but you think of her
and I of him.

Yes we each loved another.
Times have moved on.
Ask me just once, I'll go with you.
I'll be packed up and gone.
With nothing in my pockets but bluejohn.

Spinster

This
is no way to go on.
Get wise. Accept. Be
a spinster of this parish.
My life's in shards.
I will keep fit in leotards.
Go vegetarian. Accept.
Support good causes.
Be frugal, circumspect.
Keep cats. Take
tidy fits.
Go to evening classes.
Keep a nest-egg in the bank.
Try yoga. Cut your losses.
Accept. Admit you're a bit of a crank.
Oh I
may be a bit of a crank
but still I get by, frugally. Think positive.
I live and let live. Depend
on nobody. Accept.
Go in for self improvement.
Keep up with trends
I'll cultivate my conversation, I'll
cultivate my friends.
I'll grow a herbaceous border.
By hook, by crook, I'll get my house in order.

The Offering

Never in a month of them
would you go back.
Sunday,
the late smell of bacon
then the hard small feeling
of the offering in the mitten.
Remember how the hat-elastic cut.

Oh the boredom,
and how a lick of spittle
got purple dye or pink
from the hymn-book you worried.
Maybe your neighbour would
have technicoloured pictures of
Jesus curing lepers
between the frail tissue pages of her bible
or she'd stroke you with the velvet
of a pressed rosepetal
till someone sucking peppermint
and smelling of mothball
poked you and hissed
that you weren't to fidget.
Remember the singing
(with words and actions)
and how you never quite
understood the one about Nic-
odemus Coming to the Lord by Night.

And afterwards you
could play (but you
couldn't get your bike out)
and you had to keep your clothes clean.
Although there was a drying wind, no washing
flapped on the green.
So you stood behind the privet
watching girls in white net dresses
left from First Communions
birl like ballerinas
and play at heathen peever.
Perhaps an auntie
would visit with a cousin.
Everyone would eat ice-cream
and your mothers would compare you,
they'd stand you by the doorstep
and measure you up.

Later in the evening
there'd maybe be a Brethren Meeting.

Plain women wearing hats to cover
uncut hair.
Singing under lamp-posts out in our street!
And the leader (local coal-man)
shouted the odds on Armageddon,
tried to sell Salvation.
Everybody turned their televisions up.

Never in a month of them
should you go back.
Fond hope.
You'll still find you do not measure up.
The evangelist still mouths behind glass unheard.
You'll still not understand
the singing, the action or the word.
Ice-cream will cloy, too sweet, too bland.
And the offering
still hard and knotted in your hand.

Local Colour

Something I'm not familiar with, the tune
of their talking, comes tumbling before them
down the stairs which (oh I forgot) it was my turn
to do again this week.
My neighbour and my neighbour's child. I nod, we're not
on speaking terms exactly.

I don't know much about her. Her dinners smell
different. Her husband's a busdriver,
so I believe.
She carries home her groceries in Grandfare bags
though I've seen her once or twice around the corner
at Shastri's for spices and such.
(I always shop there—he's open till all hours
making good.) How does she feel?
Her children grow up with foreign accents,
swearing in fluent Glaswegian. Her face
is sullen. Her coat is drab plaid, hides

but for a hint at the hem, her sari's
gold embroidered gorgeousness. She has
a jewel in her nostril.
The golden hands with the almond nails
that push the pram turn blue
in this city's cold climate.

Obituary

We two in W.2.
walking
and all the W.2. ladies, their
hair coiffed and corrugated come
with well-done faces from the hairdressers.
We together
laughing
in our snobbery of lovers
at their narrow vowels
and strange permed poodles.
Locked too long in love, our eyes
were unaccustomed to the common place.
　　　Seems silly now really.

We two in W.2.
walking
down Byres Road
passing unconcerned
a whole florist's
full of funerals,
the nightmare butcher's shop's
unnumbered horrors,
the hung fowls
and the cold fish
dead on the slab.
We saw ourselves duplicated
by the dozen in the chainstore
with no crisis of identity.
Headlines on newsagent's placards
caused us no alarm.

Sandwichman's prophecies of doom
just slid off our backs.
The television showroom's window
showed us cities burning
in black and white but we
had no flicker of interest.
An ambulance charged screaming past
but all we noticed was the funny old
Saturday street musician.
     Seems silly now really.

We two one Sunday
at the art galleries
looking only at each other.
We two one Sunday
in the museum—
wondering why the ownership of a famous man
should make a simple object a museum piece—
and I afraid
to tell you how
sometimes I did not wash your coffee cup for days,
or touched the books you lent me
when you did not want to read.
Well, even at the time
     that seemed a bit silly really.

Christmas found me
with other fond and foolish girls
at the menswear counters
shopping for the ties that bind.
March found me
guilty of too much hope.
     Seems silly now really.

WILLIAM McILVANNEY

Stonemason

Here where the green apprentice summer
Lacquers the hedgerows,
Makes an experimental shade,
Practises the dipping plover,
The grass's blade, the rose's reason,
The mason drives his stony trade.
Death's never out of season.

Nor think his fingers contradict
The bannered birds in flight.
The fish that spawn among the reeds
The boys that blow about like seeds
And he write the same edict
Of the sun. The splintered light
And chiselled words are one.

He is as much this summer day
Chipping words in stone
As the gold coins of sunlight in the leaves.
Summer and we are masons of our own
And write our dying across every day.
Ours are the names he carves.
Mason and we are one.

Or This Man

Or this man, dressed in ash,
His cigarette ruddering through the evening.
From a distance you can see
The hands' complicated dedication
As if trying to unbutton the air,
The mouth's postures, bellowing silence,
The eyes poaching in alcohol.

Nearer, the fierce benignity of his bragging
Catches you. No name he mentions
Avoids strange laurels—an extra toe,
Incredible weight at birth, exotic death.
He introduces you to wild vision,
His eye descends on you like a plastic surgeon.

Later, his talk becomes recital,
Aspiring to mouth music.
He is, he says, 'festooned with friends'.

Once I had to take him home,
His feet knitting a strange pattern,
The hearth a dead Vesuvius of ash,
The windows cataracts, the floor his wardrobe,
The whole place dank as a cave.
No light—and we jammed a halfpenny in the meter.
He went to bed with his hat and jacket on.

I turned to say goodnight across a desert
And caught his benedictions in the gloom.
He sat propped on his pillow, blessing void,
Like a saint, not serving any purpose,
Not to be taken seriously
Because he has granted absolution to the world.

In the Library

In the library the first time
I stood in a pool of awe.
Wonder for taking, acres of promises.
The lady with the specs
And the hair-tuft on her cheek
Asking me if I had washed my hands.
The holy ritual of the water—what was this?
Superstitious as a Goth, I grabbed and ran.
At the bus-stop I discovered I had looted
A book about a girls' school. It was good.

Ridiculous, small moment but it stays.
Seed of an anger perennially mine.
The hope I lugged to that place
Back and forth and afterwards
Brought to how many books . . .
Raising my eyes
From several million pages I have seen
That small boy standing there.

The time it took
The fields there were to cut, the loads to carry
Hutches to be filled
The roads to lay
The tired nights in narrow beds, the rage
To bring him to his patch of floor,
His eyes like begging bowls.

I don't forgive
The determined absence of himself he was to find.
The self-perpetuating silliness, the cliques
Of convoluted silences, the lies,
The long articulate anathema
Against him and his pals.
They were nowhere to be seen unless those bits
Between the lines and down the edges
Were for them.

No wonder they drew graffiti in the margins.

Suicide

And there was one blinded by private grief
Of death or distance, for three days read himself
Dimly on the rough braille of his life,
Sealed door and pane against the summer's breath,
Lay down and bought a shillingsworth of death.
The hat went round the street to help his wife.

Outside his window a world rehearsed in public
For a future not assured. Asia bled
Prophetically. American wives
Lay fearfully in laundered single beds.
Old Europe nursed her gangrene and was sick.
The price of watching them was private lives.

His temerity bemused us. Yet we gave
Our coins in tribute to old-fashioned style
That against a world professional in wars,
Skilled in converting a city to a grave,
Dared challenge Dachau and to us bequeath
His delicately wrought, small, hand-made death.

Death of the Hare

Death of the hare
That Sunday of sky,
Shot with river and leaves.

I was such an apprentice among them,
Those big men muffled in incomprehensible talk,
Their laughter a bright ball thrown
I never could catch.
Copying strides, I was even learning to walk.

Those were the first of my fields—
The horse reined with its fright,
The river tasting of rust,
The sun breaking in showers from the leaves,
The bee loud as a plane, the aeroplane quiet as a bee.
Step by step I was learning.

Explosion of chase:
The dogs took us with them
On tautening wires of wind,
Pulled me out through my mouth in a shout.

It was caught.
I rushed to the middle
Of whatever would happen.
The men gathered casually round,
Made a core for my day.
My eyes moved like a ferret among them.
They talked dogs.
Some already were moving away.

One took a whimper of fur in his hands,
I hung by the ears.
Turning absently into the sun,
His hands rickled its back
And it swung,
Swung, swings

Still in shimmer of sun,
Black in fields that don't change.
Putrefaction of mind.

Incident

'Watch yer caur fur a tanner, mister.' Strange
As hieroglyphs the words froze in his breath.
His eyes rifled the passing faces deftly, trained
To pick each moment's pockets of small change.
Thin body in its trousers of frail cloth,
Elbowless jersey, cracking shoes, attained
An emblematic stance, defying pity.
Like a confidential file his starved face read
'Congenital case of backstreets of a city'
While Glasgow suppurated round his head.

The man looked down, feeling his well made suit
Grow luxuriously heavy. That raw face
Formed in his glance a chance cast of bleak bones
(Life throws them casually before our feet)
Where the future had already taken place.
While the dark street bled infection from its stones.

His thumb traced on a coin his indecision.
Drop a sixpence in a scummy wishing-well?
His wife's voice—sacrificial, cold precision:
'Tell the little brat to go to Hell.'

They wandered in a maze of ideal homes,
Kitchen units, cookers, and hi-fis.
Welfare Wonderland had come to Kelvin Hall.
Racked by the cost of carpeting two rooms,
His wife struggled with their stern economies.
(Necessity makes martyrs of us all.)
But tasting dishes, testing heaters, he
Astigmatically saw one clenched grey face
Superimposed on chair, wood fireplace.
And all it said relentlessly was 'Me'.

That night he dreamed a different exhibition—
Stands where children advertised the sores
Of other people's failure. Bargain schemes
In which injustice was the prime condition.
Mock rooms with plush indifference on their floors.
Comfort that was fuelled on warm dreams
Of everything's vague rightness. And he heard
Coming from places that he could not see
Insistent as canned music, the soft words:
'Nothing can be real that counts out me.'

But routine brings us to serenity.
Next morning he ate well, washed down the car
And paused, shocked to see scraped across his boot
With stone or knife a brief obscenity,
Blemishing his wellbeing like a scar
Of violence that was to come. He took
A tube of matching paint, healed it but could
Feel malice mounting still like a thrombosis
Unseen, implicit with tomorrow's blood.
Aloes on nails do not cure a neurosis.

Eugenesis

On the first day They eradicated war.
Nations were neutralized. In desert places
The cumbered void rusted with defused bombs,
The gutted chambers. In random heaps
The rockets lay, like molar monuments
To brontosauri sentenced to extinction.

On the second day They fed the starving.
The capsules gave immunity from hunger.
Faces filled. The smiles were uniform.
The computers had found a formula for plenty.

The third day ended work. With summer
Processed to a permanence, the sun-
Machine in operation, every day
Would be as long as They desired it.
Season-chambers were erected. The nostalgic
Could take a holiday to autumn if they wished.
The computers thought of everything.

On the fourth day death was dead.
Synthetic hearts, machine-tooled brains,
Eyes and limbs were all expendable.
Immortality came wrapped in polythene.
Every face was God's you saw upon the street.

By the fifth day crime was cured.
Mind-mechanics, They located every hatred,
Extracted it, and amputated angers.
Each idea was sterilized before its issue.
The computers fixed a safety-mark for thinking.

The sixth day saw heaven's inauguration.
Benignity pills were issued. Kindness meetings
Were held on every corner. They declared
Love as the prerogative of all.
That day became the longest there had been.
But as long as there was light the people smiled.

On the seventh day, while They were resting
A small man with red hair had disappeared.
A museum missed a tent. Neither was found.
He left an immortal wife, the changeless years
Of endless happiness, and a strange note
In ancient script, just four historic letters.
The Autotongue translated: 'Irrational Anger.'
The Medic Machine advised: 'Rejection Symptoms.
Source Unknown. Primordial and Contagious.'

It was too late. The word ran like a rash
On walls and daubed on doorways. Cities emptied.
In panic They neglected Their machines.
The sunset was unauthorized. Its beauty
Triggered the light-oriented metal cocks
That crew until their mechanisms burst.
Fires twinkled in the new night, shaping mattocks.
On the dark hills an unheavenly sound was heard.
The Historometer intoned into the silence:
'Ancient Barbaric Custom Known as Laughter.'
Seizing up, the computers began to cry.

Grandmother

By the time I knew my grandmother she was dead.
Before that she was where I thought she stood,
Spectacles, slippers, venerable head,
A standard-issue twinkle in her eyes—
Familiar stage-props of grandmotherhood.
It took her death to teach me they were lies.

My sixteen-year-old knowingness was shocked
To hear her family narrate her past
In quiet nostalgic chorus. As they talked
Her body stiffened on the muted fast
Though well washed linen coverlet of her bed.
The kitchen where we sat, a room I knew,
Took on a strangeness with each word they said.
How she was born where wealth was pennies, grew

Into a woman before she was a girl,
From dirt and pain constructed happiness,
Shed youth's dreams in the fierce sweat of a mill,
Married and mothered in her sixteenth year,
Fed children from her own mouth's emptiness
In an attic rats owned half of, liked her beer.
Careless, they scattered pictures: mother, wife,
Strikes lived through, hard concessions bought and sold
In a level-headed bargaining with life,
Told anecdotes in which her strength rang gold,
Her eyes were clear, her wants as plain as salt.
The past became a mint from which they struck
Small change till that room glittered like a vault.
The corpse in the other room became to me
Awesome as Pharaoh now, as if one look
Would show me all that I had failed to see.

The kitchen became museum in my sight,
Sacred as church. These were the very chairs
In which her gnarled dignity grew frail.
Her hard-won pride had kept these brasses bright.
Her tireless errands were etched upon the stairs.
A vase shone in the sun, holy as grail.
I wanted to bring others to this room,
Say it's nothing else than this that people mean,
A place to which humility can come,
A wrested niche where no one else has been
Won from the wastes of broken worlds and worse.
Here we can stay. Stupid and false, of course.
Themselves to the living is all we have to give.

Let this be
To her, for wreath, gift, true apology.

EDWIN MORGAN

A Child's Coat of Many Colours

love	head	eyes	bawl	bend	wake	feet	wink	soap
come	yell	nose	soul	rest	tell	wash	poop	bath
rose	kiss	look	bell	days	howl	wind	sulk	talc
baby	rusk	lips	arms	mole	neck	back	tail	talk
hand	hold	room	gaze	want	wall	tale	seat	mama
		blue	bird	purr	burp	dada		
		toys	crib	pram	tree	walk		
		milk	suck	pins	grin	pink		
		hair	pond	bark	crow	wish		
		dogs	wait	mash	glad	slop		
		last	home	ring	next	road		
		feed	wean	fire	this	shop		
		that	bead	poke	soft	tear		
		push	risk	wipe	blub	hoop		
		rash	clap	skip	lull	sing		
		skin	doll	girl	lift	song		
		ears	boys	slip	star	trip		
		moon	park	rain	roof	boat		
		fist	gate	ball	leaf	duck		
		step	grip	sand	bite	dusk		
		take	pail	dawn	gums	chum		
		wave	noon	stir	fork	shoe		
		toes	gold	stop	warm	blow		
		give	puss	call	pony	wail		
		turn	knee	slap	puke	suds		
		lean		open		shut		
		year		dear		fall		
		wrap		rock		down		
		good		snap		mine		
		week		true		trot		

Glasgow 5 March 1971

With a ragged diamond
of shattered plate-glass
a young man and his girl
are falling backwards into a shop-window.
The young man's face
is bristling with fragments of glass
and the girl's leg has caught
on the broken window
and spurts arterial blood
over her wet-look white coat.
Their arms are starfished out
braced for impact,
their faces show surprise, shock,
and the beginning of pain.
The two youths who have pushed them
are about to complete the operation
reaching into the window
to loot what they can smartly.
Their faces show no expression.
It is a sharp clear night
in Sauchiehall Street.
In the background two drivers
keep their eyes on the road.

Fallin Stirlingshire October 1970

A man has thrown his collie into the dustbin
outside his house. The dog
has been struck by a car.
He glances briefly into the bin
before he bangs down the lid:
the animal is whimpering and scuffling, already
it has half sunk into the ashes.
In the background the man's wife
looks coldly from the window, approving.

Germany December 1970

A dead man is driving an old Mercedes
straight at a brick wall.
He is only one hour dead,
his hands have been laid
realistically on the wheel
by Herr Rudi Ulenhaut
the development engineer.
Under his dropped jaw
an inflatable safety air bag,
waiting to be tested on impact,
has just flown up
and broken his neck.

The Woman

A string of pearls
in the dark window, that wet spring,
sometimes a white hand raised with a cigarette
blurred by rain and buses
anyhow. A lonely
ring.

Nothing she was waiting for
came, unless what took her
in the coldest arms.

It seems to be the pearls
we remember, for what they spoke
of another life than waiting,
and being unknown dying
in a high dark street.

Who she was you'll keep thinking.
The hearse rolled off in thunder,
but showers only lay dust.

Clydesdale

go
    fetlocksnow
          go
            gullfurrow
               go

go
    brassglow
          go
            sweatflow
               go

go
    plodknow
          go
            clodshow
               go

go
    leatherbelow
          go
            potatothrow
               go

go
    growfellow
          go
            crowfollow
               go

go
    Balerno
          go
            Palermo
               whoa

For Bonfires

1

The leaves are gathered, the trees are dying
for a time.
A seagull cries through white smoke in the garden fires
that fill the heavy air.
All day heavy air
is burning, a moody dog
sniffs and circles the swish of the rake.
In streaks of ash, the gardener drifting
ghostly, beats his hands, a cloud
of breath to the red sun.

2

An island in the city, happy demolition men
behind windowed hoardings—look at them
trailing drills through rubble dust, kicking rubble,
smoking leaning on a pick, putting the stub
over an ear and the hot yellow helmet over that,
whistling up the collapsing chimney, kicking the
ricochet, rattling the trail with
snakes of wire, slamming slabs
down, plaster, cornice, brick, brick
on broken brick and plaster dust,
sprawling with steaming cans and pieces
at noon, afternoon bare sweat shining
paths down chalky backs, coughing
in filtered sunshine, slithering, swearing,
joking, slowly stacking and building
their rubbish into a total bonfire.
Look at that Irishman, bending
in a beautiful arc to throw
the last black rafter to the top,
stands back, walks round it singing
as it crackles into flame—old doors,
old beams, boxes, window-frames,
a rag doll, sacks, flex, old newspapers,
burst shelves, a shoe, old dusters, rags of
wallpaper roses. And they all stand round,
and cheer the tenement to smoke.

3

In a galvanized bucket
the letters burn. They roar and twist
and the leaves curl back one by one.
They put out claws and scrape the iron
like a living thing,
but the scrabbling to be free soon subsides.
The black pages are fused
to a single whispering mass
threaded by dying tracks of gold.
Let them grow cold,
and when they're dead
quickly draw breath.

Ellingham Suffolk January 1972

Below a water-mill at midnight
breaking the river Waveney into white
an intricate water-dance of forty-one swans
and one man leaning from the mill window
smokes and broods
ravished and nothing understood.

Death in Duke Street

A huddle on the greasy street—
cars stop, nose past, withdraw—
dull glint on soles of tackety boots,
frayed rough blue trousers, nondescript coat
stretching back, head supported
in strangers' arms, a crowd collecting—
'Whit's wrang?' 'Can ye see'm?'
'An auld fella, he's had it.'
On one side, a young mother in a headscarf
is kneeling to comfort him, her three-year-old son
stands puzzled, touching her coat, her shopping-bag
spills its packages that people look at
as they look at everything. On the other side

a youth, nervous, awkwardly now
at the centre of attention as he shifts his arm
on the old man's shoulders, wondering
what to say to him, glancing up at the crowd.
These were next to him when he fell,
and must support him into death.
He seems not to be in pain,
he is speaking slowly and quietly
but he does not look at any of them,
his eyes are fixed on the sky,
already he is moving out
beyond everything belonging.
As if he still belonged
they hold him very tight.

Only the hungry ambulance
howls for him through the staring squares.

Grierson

Then the nets rose and fell
in the swell. Then the dark water
went fiery suddenly, then black.
Then with a haul it was all
fire, all silver fire
fighting down the black. Then the fire
rose in the air slowly,
struggling over the side of the boat.
Then it was deck and hold.
Then it was the dance of death
in silver with grey gulls.
Then it was low clouds, bars of light,
high water slapping, choppy wake
and oilskin tea then.

Glasgow October 1972

At the Old Ship Bank pub in Saltmarket
a milk-lapping contest is in progress.
A dozen very assorted Bridgeton cats
have sprung from their starting-blocks
to get their heads down in the gleaming saucers.
In the middle of the picture
young Tiny is about to win his bottle of whisky
by kittening through the sweet half-gill
in one minute forty seconds flat, but
Sarah, at the end of the line,
self-contained and silver-grey,
has sat down with her back to the saucer
and surveys the photographers calmly.
She is a cat who does not like milk.

Glasgow Sonnets

I

A mean wind wanders through the backcourt trash.
Hackles on puddles rise, old mattresses
puff briefly and subside. Play-fortresses
of brick and bric-a-brac spill out some ash.
Four storeys have no windows left to smash,
but in the fifth a chipped sill buttresses
mother and daughter the last mistresses
of that black block condemned to stand, not crash.
Around them the cracks deepen, the rats crawl.
The kettle whimpers on a crazy hob.
Roses of mould grow from ceiling to wall.
The man lies late since he has lost his job,
smokes on one elbow, letting his coughs fall
thinly into an air too poor to rob.

III

'See a tenement due for demolition?
I can get ye rooms in it, two, okay?
Seven hundred and nothin legal to pay

for it's no legal, see? That's my proposition,
ye can take it or leave it but. The position
is simple, you want a hoose, I say
for eight hundred pound it's yours.' And they,
trailing five bairns, accepted his omission
of the foul crumbling stairwell, windows wired
not glazed, the damp from the canal, the cooker
without pipes, packs of rats that never tired—
any more than the vandals bored with snooker
who stripped the neighbouring houses, howled, and fired
their aerosols—of squeaking 'Filthy lucre!'

Acknowledgments

The compilers and publishers are grateful to the following for permission to reproduce poems:

STEWART CONN for 'Choral Symphony', 'Winter', 'Aldridge Pond' and 'In the Kibble Palace'.

HUTCHINSON PUBLISHING GROUP LTD and STEWART CONN for 'Tremors', 'Portents', 'Forbears', 'On Craigie Hill', 'To My Father', 'Reiteration' and 'Family Visit' from *An Ear to the Ground*.

DOUGLAS DUNN for 'Wedding'.

FABER & FABER LTD and DOUGLAS DUNN for 'Ships', 'Bring Out Your Dead', 'Men of Terry Street', 'A Removal from Terry Street' and 'The Silences' all from *Terry Street*; 'White Fields', 'Boys with Coats' and 'The Competition' all from *Love or Nothing*; 'After the War' from *The Happier Life*.

TOM LEONARD for 'Poetry', 'Words for E.', 'A Summer's Day', 'The Appetite', 'Moral Philosophy', 'The Good Thief', 'Fireworks', 'Yon Night', 'Jiss Ti Lit Yi No', 'The Dropout', 'Paroakial', 'The Qualification' and 'The Other Side of the Ticket'.

LIZ LOCHHEAD for 'Lady of Shalott', 'Bawd', 'Song', 'My Rival's House', 'Bluejohn Pockets', 'Spinster' and 'The Offering'.

GORDON WRIGHT PUBLISHING and LIZ LOCHHEAD for 'Local Colour' and 'Obituary' from *Memo for Spring* by Liz Lochhead.

WILLIAM MCILVANNEY for 'Or This Man', 'In the Library' and 'Death of a Hare'.

EYRE METHUEN and WILLIAM MCILVANNEY for 'Stonemason', 'Suicide', 'Incident', 'Eugenesis' and 'Grandmother' all from *The Langships in Harbour*.

EDWIN MORGAN for 'A Child's Coat of Many Colours', 'For Bonfires', 'Grierson' and 'Glasgow October 1972'.

CARCANET PRESS for 'The Woman', 'Death in Duke Street' and 'Glasgow Sonnets I and III' all from *From Glasgow to Saturn* by Edwin Morgan.

AKROS for 'Clydesdale' by Edwin Morgan from *The Horseman's Word*.

IAN MCKELVIE for 'Glasgow 5 March 1971', 'Fallin Stirlingshire October 1970', 'Germany December 1970' and 'Ellingham Suffolk January 1972' all from *Instamatic Poems* by Edwin Morgan.